Easy Way To
KOREAN CONVERSATION
한국어 회화

THIRD REVISED EDITION

by
Pong Kook Lee
Chi Sik Ryu
Professors of Yonsei University

With Cassette Tape

Recording Voices:
Mr. K. J. Lee, Mr. H. C. Kim, Miss K.B. Jeon & Mrs. Bland

HOLLYM
Elizabeth, NJ · Seoul

Easy Way to Korean Conversation

Copyright © 1976, 1982, 1984, 1999
by Hollym Corporation; Publishers

All rights reserved.

First published in 1976
by Hollym Corporation; Publishers

Third revised edition, 1984
Twelfth printing, 1996
Fourth revised edition, 1999
Third printing, 2004
by Hollym International Corp.
18 Donald Place, Elizabeth. New Jersey 07208 U.S.A
Phone: (908)353-1655   Fax: (908)353-0255
http://www.hollym.com

Published simultaneously in Korea
by Hollym Corporation; Publishers
7th floor. Core Building, 13-13 Gwancheol-dong, Jongno-gu,
Seoul 110-111, Korea
Phone: (02) 735-7551~4   Fax: (02) 730-5149, 8192
http://www.hollym.co.kr

ISBN: 0-930878-17-5

Printed in Korea

PREFACE

Welcome to Korea!

We sincerely hope that your stay in Korea will be as comfortable and as pleasant as possible.

Now, to help you to converse more easily and catch some of the excitement of talking to Koreans, we have prepared this booklet accompanied by lively voices recorded on a 60-minute cassette tape which will give you some true pictures of spoken Korean.

Just play the tape on your recorder and look through the text.

You will certainly begin to pick up some most urgently needed words and expressions. Korean has levels of speech according to the politeness used. We have tried to use the formal educated level of speech through out, so even if you hear slightly different expressions in actual conversation, they are nothing but short forms or speech form on different levels.

Of course, this short course is not meant to be comprehensive, and would be most helpful if you have a Korean friend to help you. Also in order to help you with a little more knowledge of Korean language and culture, we have added a few pages of handy references in the appendix.

The romanization of the Korean alphabet in the text (see Appendix 1) follows the system adopted by the Ministry of Education of the Republic of Korea which accommodates McCune Reischauer system with minor revision. The pronunciation guide (see Appendix 2) will give you some guidelines, but why not just learn the Korean alphabet directly? It can be done in less than half an hour! Our efforts will be amply rewarded if this small presentation forms the foundation for your learning our language.

P. K. Lee

C. S. Ryu

CONTENTS

Preface

PART I BASIC WORDS AND EXPRESSIONS

1. Greetings and Leave Takings ....[Cassette—Side A]...9
2. Affirmative and Negative Expressions 11
   (1) Affirmatives 11
   (2) Negatives 12
3. Questions and Imperatives 14
   (1) Questions 14
   (2) Imperatives 16
4. Numerals, Calendars and Time 17
   (1) Numerals 17
   (2) Calendars 18
   (3) Time 20
5. Additional Words and Expressions 22

PART II EVERYDAY CONVERSATION

1. Introduction ....[Cassette—Side B]...29
2. Invitation 31
3. Visit 33
4. Asking for Information 35

5.	Getting around in Town	38
	(1) Taxi	38
	(2) Bus	39
	(3) Subway	40
6.	Shopping	42
	(1) At a Department Store	42
	(2) At a Souvenir Shop	43
7.	Telephone	45
8.	At a Tearoom	47
9.	At a Palace	49
10.	At a Pavilion	51
11.	At a Hotel	53
12.	At a Restaurant	55
13.	At the Post Office	58

APPENDIX — *TO HELP UNDERSTAND KOREA*

1.	Romanization of the Korean Alphabet	63
2.	The Korean Alphabet and Pronunciation	66
3.	Land and People	70
4.	History	71
5.	Holidays	73
6.	A Few More Interesting Points	75

Modern Seoul

PART I
BASIC WORDS AND EXPRESSIONS

1. Greetings and Leave Takings

1. How do you do?
   How are you?

2. Good morning.
   Good afternoon.
   Good evening.

3. I'm glad to see you.

4. Mr. Kim.

5. Miss Kang.

6. Mrs. Park.[3]

1. Annyŏnghashimnikka?
   안 녕 하 십 니 까 ?[1]

2. Annyŏnghashimnikka?
   안 녕 하 십 니 까 ?

3. Manna poeŏ pan-gapsŭmnida.
   만 나 뵈 어 반 갑 습 니 다.

4. Kim sŏnsaengnim.
   김 선 생 님.[2]

5. Kang yang.
   강 양.

6. Pak yŏsa.
   박 여 사.

---

(1) Most Western greetings could be expressed by "*Annyŏnghashimnikka?*" (안녕하십니까 ?) or by its short form "*Annyŏnghaseyo?*" (안녕하세요 ?)
'Hello' used on the telephone conversation is "*Yŏboseyo.*" (여보세요)

(2) The traditional form for addressing a person in Korean is the person's title + *nim* (님) or the name + *ssi* (씨) for either a man or a woman, and the surname + *puin* (부인) for a married woman. Modern usage is not entirely fixed yet, but the full name + *ssi* (씨), title + *nim* (님) or *sŏnsaengnim* (선생님) are always acceptable

Part I
Cassette—Side A

7. Professor Lee.

7. I kyosunim.
이 교 수 님.

8. Doctor Choe.

8. Ch'oe paksanim.
최 박 사 님.

9. President Im.

9. Im sajangnim.
임 사 장 님.

10. Good-bye.

10. { Annyŏnghi kashipshio.
안 녕 히 가 십 시 오. (4)
Annyŏnghi kyeshipshio.
안 녕 히 계 십 시 오.

11. Good night.

11. Annyŏnghi chumushipshio.
안 녕 히 주 무 십 시 오.

12. I'll see you again.

12. Tto poepkessŭmnida.
또 뵙 겠 습 니 다. (5)

13. I'll see you soon.

13. Kot poepkessŭmnida.
곧 뵙 겠 습 니 다.

14. Remember me to Mr. Hwang.

14. Hwang sŏnsaengnimege anbu chŏnhae chuseyo.
황 선 생 님 에게 안 부 전 해 주 세 요.

for a man or a woman, the name +*yang*(양) for an unmarried girl, the name +*puin* (부인) for a married woman, and the name +*yŏsa*(여사) for a distinguished educated woman. In case of doubt, the English usage of Mr., Miss and Mrs. are quite well accepted by most Koreans. However, since Korean woman retains her surname even after her marriage, the use of Mrs. is sometimes confused.

(3) There are no set rules in spelling Korean proper names. Other Koreans spell *Park*, *Pak* or *Bag*, *Lee*, *Li* or *Yi* and sometimes *Rhee*.

(4) Literally "Go in peace." It is said by the person who is staying to the person leaving.

(5) The personal pronouns, I, you, he, they, etc. are very often omitted in Korean.

2. Affirmative and Negative Expressions
Cassette—Side A

2. Affirmative and Negative Expressions

(1) Affirmatives

1. Yes.
   Yes, certainly.

2. Oh, yes.

3. Of course.

4. Fine.
   All right.
   Very well.

5. Yes, I will.

1. Ye.
   예. (1)

2. A, ne.
   아, 네.

3. Mullonimnida.
   물 론 입 니 다. (2)

4. Chossŭmnida.
   좋 습 니 다. (3)

5. Ye, kŭrŏk'e hagessŭmnida.
   예, 그렇게 하겠 습 니 다. (4)

---

(1) *ye*(예) is standard, but *ne*(네) is quite often used, and sometimes *nye*(녜) is also heard.
(2) *mullon*(물론) alone would suffice, but "*Mullonimnida.*" (물론입니다.) is formal. "*Mullonijyo.*" (물론이죠.) may be conveniently used in conversation.
(3) Its short form is "*Choayo.*" (좋아요.)
(4) Its short form is "*Ye, kŭrŏjiyo.*" (예, 그러지요.)

Part I
Cassette—Side A

6. You're right.

6. Olssŭmnida.
   옳 습 니 다.

7. I think so.

7. Kŭrŏk'e saenggak'amnida. (5)
   그렇게 생 각 합 니 다.

(2) Negatives

1. No.

1. Anio.
   아니오.

2. Of course not.
   Certainly not.

2. Mullon animnida.
   물 론 아 닙 니 다.

3. I don't know.
   I can't understand.

3. Morŭgessŭmnida.
   모 르겠 습 니 다.

4. I don't think so.

4. Kŭrŏk'e saenggak'aji anssŭmnida.
   그렇게 생 각 하지 않 습 니 다.

5. I don't like it.

5. Choahaji anssŭmnida.
   좋 아 하지 않 습 니 다.

6. I don't want it.

6. Wŏnch'i anssŭmnida.
   원 치 않 습 니 다.

---

(5) "*Kŭrŏch'iyo.*" (그렇지요.) may also be used. In Korean, the same verbal expression is used for all persons, singular and plural, so that *-imnida* (-입니다), *-hamnida* (-합니다), *-jiyo* (-지요) etc.

2. Affirmative and Negative Expressions
Cassette—Side A

7. Not yet.

8. I'm not sure.

9. It's no use.

10. I don't agree.

11. Never mind.

12. Don't mention it.
    Not at all.
    You're welcome.

7. Ajik.
   아직, ……⁽¹⁾

8. Hwakshilch'i anssŭmnida.
   확실치않습니다.

9. P'iryoŏpsŭmnida.
   필요없습니다.

10. Ch'ansŏnghaji anssŭmnida.
    찬성하지않습니다.

11. Yŏmnyŏ mashipshio.
    염려마십시오.

12. Ch'ŏnmanŭi malssŭmimnida.
    천만의말씀입니다.

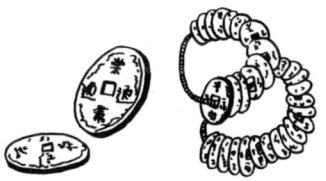

---

(1) Depending on the context used it is usually followed by a negative verb form.

3. Questions and Imperatives

(1) Questions

1. Are you Mr. Chong?

2. Is that so?

3. Do you know Miss Song?

4. Can you come[2] with me?

5. Will you do me a favor?

6. Shall we go[2] now?

7. What is your name?
   My name is Yu-jong Im.

1. Chŏng sŏnsaengnimishimnikka?
   정 선 생 님 이 십 니 까?[1]

2. Kŭrŏssŭmnikka?
   그 렇 습 니 까?

3. Song yangŭl ashimnikka?
   송 양 을 아 십 니 까?

4. Chŏwa kach'i kal su issŭmnikka?
   저 와 같 이 갈[2] 수 있 습 니 까?

5. Put'agŭl tŭrŏ chushigessŭmnikka?
   부 탁 을 들 어 주 시 겠 습 니 까?

6. Chigŭm kalkkayo?
   지 금 갈[2] 까 요?

7. Sŏnghami muŏshimnikka?
   성 함 이 무 엇 입 니 까?
   Chŏui irŭmŭn Im Yujongimnida.
   저 의 이 름 은 임 유 종 입 니 다.

---

(1) Nominative case of 'You,' *tangshini*(당신이) is almost always omitted in Korean.

(2) The root form of 'come' is *oda*(오다) and 'go' is *kada*(가다). The use of 'come' and 'go' is slightly different from that of English. The position of the speaker controls the use.

3. Questions and Imperatives
Cassette—Side A

8. Where is your office?

   It is in Chongno.

9. Who is he?

   He is my father.

10. Which is your house?

    That is my house.

11. When did you come?

    I came yesterday.

12. Why did you come late?

    I was busy.

13. How long will you stay here?

    I'll be here for a week.

8. Samushiri ŏdi issŭmnikka?
   사무실이 어디 있습니까?
   Chongno-e issŭmnida.
   종로에 있습니다.

9. Kŭbunŭn nuguimnikka?
   그 분은 누구입니까?
   Kŭbunŭn chŏŭi abŏjiimnida.
   그 분은 저의 아버지입니다.

10. Ŏnŭ chibi taegimnikka?
    어느 집이 댁입니까?
    Chŏgŏshi che chibimnida.
    저것이 제 집입니다.

11. Ŏnje osyŏssŭmnikka?
    언제 오셨습니까?
    Ojŏkke wassŭmnida.
    어저께 왔습니다.

12. Wae nŭjŏssŭmnikka?
    왜 늦었습니까?
    Pappassŭmnida.
    바빴습니다.

13. Ŏlma tongan yŏgie kyeshigessŭmnikka?
    얼마 동안 여기에 계시겠습니까?
    Han chuil tongan itkessŭmnida.
    한 주일 동안 있겠습니다.

Part I
Cassette—Side A

14. Whose car is this?

    It is my car.

15. Who(m) did you meet?

    I met Miss Yang.

14. Igŏsŭn nŭguŭi ch'aimnikka?
    이것은 누구의⁽⁴⁾ 차 입 니 까?⁽⁵⁾
    Che ch'aimnida.
    제   차 입 니 다.

15. Nugurŭl mannassŭmnikka?
    누 구 를 만 났 습 니 까?
    Misŭ Yangŭl mannassŭmnida.
    미 스 양 을 만 났 습 니 다.

(2) Imperatives

1. Please come this way.

2. Go that way.

3. Please sit down.

4. Help yourself.

5. Please show me.

1. Iriro oshipshio.
   이 리 로 오 십 시 오.

2. Chŏriro kashipshio.
   저 리 로 가 십 시 오.

3. Anjŭshipshio.
   앉 으 십 시 오.

4. Tŭshipshio.
   드   십 시 오.

5. Poyŏ chushipshio.
   보 여 주 십 시 오.

---

(4) Modifier precedes subject, object or predicative noun.

    nominative → 이 (*i*), 가 (*ka*)   genitive → 의 (*ŭi*)
    accusative → 을 (*ŭl*), 를 (*rŭl*)   dative → 에 (*e*), 에게 (*ege*)

(5) The word order in a typical Korean sentence is subject first and predicate last, with object or complement in between.

    이것은 + 누구의 차 + 입니까?   (나는) + 어저께 + 왔습니다.
    This   whose car   is?   (I)   yesterday   came.

4. Numerals, [1] Calendars and Time

(1) Numerals

1. How many are there?

2. There are two.

3. How many persons are there?

4. There are four persons.

5. How much is it?

6. It's ten won.

7. How much do you want?

8. I want three kilograms of it.

1. Myŏch'i issŭmnikka?
   몇 이 있습니까?

2. Turi issŭmnida.
   둘이 있습니다.

3. Myŏt sarami issŭmnikka?
   몇 사람이있습니까?

4. Ne sarami issŭmnida.
   네 사람이있습니다.

5. Ŏlmaimnikka?
   얼마입니까?

6. Shibwŏnimnida.
   10 원입니다.

7. Ŏlmana wŏnhashimnikka?
   얼마나 원하십니까?

8. Sam k'illo chushipshio.
   3 킬로주십시오.

---

(1) Individual Korean words are like Chinese without any genders, case or numbers. The gender is expressed by a character-prefix denoting sex and then used only when quite necessary; the case is expressed by particles known as postposition, and number by adding another particle denoting plural number.

(2) Calendars

1. What day of the week is it today?

2. It's Wednesday.

1. Onŭri musŭn yoirimnikka?
   오늘이 무슨 요일입니까?

2. Suyoirimnida.
   수요일입니다.

Number[1]	Korean		Chinese Derivative		Number	Korean		Chinese Derivative	
1.	hana	하나	il	일	11.	yŏrhana	열하나	shibil	십일
2.	tul	둘	i	이	12.	yŏltul	열둘	shibi	십이
3.	set	셋	sam	삼	20.	sŭmŭl	스물	iship	이십
4.	net	넷	sa	사	30.	sŏrŭn	서른	samship	삼십
5.	tasŏt	다섯	o	오	40.	mahŭn	마흔	saship	사십
6.	yŏsŏt	여섯	yuk	육	50.	shwin	쉰	oship	오십
7.	ilgop	일곱	ch'il	칠	100.	paek	백	(il)paek	(일)백
8.	yŏdŏl	여덟	p'al	팔	1,000.	ch'ŏn	천	(il)ch'ŏn	(일)천
9.	ahop	아홉	ku	구	10,000.	man	만	(il)man	(일)만
10.	yŏl	열	ship	십	100,000.	shimman	십만	shimman	십만

Example 1: 325 sambaegisbibo
삼백이십오

Example 2: 15,800 manoch'ŏnp'albaek
만 오천 팔백

(1) There are two systems to count numbers, that is, Korean and Chinese derivative. The latter is usually used in counting things in successive order, such as counting days, money or mileage, etc.

4. Numerals, Calendars and Time
Cassette—Side A

3. What day (of the month) is it today?

4. It's May 7.

5. It's Saturday October 12.

6. What season do you like?

7. I like autumn.

3. Onŭri myŏch'irimnikka?
   오늘이 며 칠 입 니 까?

4. Owŏl ch'iririmnida.
   5 월 7일입니다.

5. Shiwŏl shibiil t'oyoirimnida.
   10 월 12 일 토요일입니다.

6. Ŏnŭ kyejŏrŭl choahashimnikka?
   어느 계 절 을 좋아하십 니 까?

7. Kaŭrŭl choahamnida.
   가 을 을 좋아 합 니 다.

Weekdays:	Sunday	*iryoil* 일요일	Monday	*woryoil* 월요일	Tuesday	*hwayoil* 화요일
	Wednesday	*suyoil* 수요일	Thursday	*mogyoil* 목요일	Friday	*kŭmyoil* 금요일
	Saturday	*t'oyoil* 토요일				
Months:	January	*irwŏl* 1월	February	*iwŏl* 2월	March	*samwŏl* 3월
	April	*sawŏl* 4월	May	*owŏl* 5월	June	*yuwŏl* 6월
	July	*ch'irwŏl* 7월	August	*p'arwŏl* 8월	September	*kuwŏl* 9월
	October	*shiwŏl* 10월	November	*shibirwŏl* 11월	December	*shibiwŏl* 12월
Seasons:	Spring *pom* (봄)		Summer *yŏrŭm* (여름)		Autumn (Fall) *kaŭl* (가을)	Winter *kyŏul* (겨울)

Part I
Cassette—Side A

(3) Time

1. What time is it?

2. It's eight o'clock.

3. When shall we meet?

4. Let's meet at nine fifteen.

1. Myŏt shiimnikka?
   몇 시⁽¹⁾입니까?

2. Yŏdŏlshiimnida.
   8 시 입니다.

3. Ŏnje mannalkkayo?
   언제 만날까요?

4. Ahopshi shibobuneyo.
   9 시 15 분에요.

(ahopshi shibobun)   (hanshi)   (tushi)   (seshi)

(1) Time: one o'clock—*hanshi* (1시)   two o'clock—*tushi* (2시)   three o'clock—*seshi* (3시)
five minutes after four—*neshi obun* (4시 5분)   fifteen minutes after five—*tasŏssi shibobun* (5시 15분)
thirty minutes after six—*yŏsŏssi samshippun* (6시 30분)   half past five—*tasŏssi pan* (5시 반)
forty minutes after six—*yŏsŏssi sashippun* (6시 40분)   ten o'clock—*yŏlshi* (10시)
eleven o'clock—*yŏrhanshi* (11시)   twelve o'clock—*yŏltushi* (12시)
A.M.—*ojŏn* (오전)   P.M.—*ohu* (오후)   night—*pam* (밤)

4. Numerals, Calendars and Time
Cassette—Side A

5. When do you leave?

6. I leave at eleven and a half.

5. Ŏnje ttŏnashimnikka?
   언제떠나십니까?

6. Yŏrhanshi pane ttŏnamnida.
   11시 반에 떠납니다.

Units:	money—*wŏn*(원)	person—*saram, pun*(사람, 분)	animal—*mari*(마리)
	thing—*kae*(개)	sheet—*chang*(장)	book—*kwŏn*(권)
	hour—*shigan*(시간)	minute—*pun*(분)	month—*tal*(달)
	cup—*chan*(잔)	age—*sal or se*(살, 세)	car—*tae*(대)
	Example: 5 person—*tasŏt saram*		620 wŏn—*yukpaegishibwŏn*
	다섯 사람		육백 이십 원

Tourist Bureau

Part I
Cassette—Side A

5. Additional Words and Expressions

— A —

1. How is your family?
2. Please remember me to your wife.
3. I'm an American.
4. I cannot speak Korean.
5. You are Koreans.
6. Can you speak English?
7. He's not an American.

1. Kajogŭn chal chinaeshimnikka?
   가족은 잘 지내십니까?
2. Puinege anbu chŏnhae chuseyo.
   부인에게 안부 전해 주세요.
3. Chŏnŭn Miguk saramimnida.
   저는 미국 사람입니다.
4. Chŏnŭn Han-gugŏrŭl mot'amnida.
   저는 한국어를 못합니다.
5. Yŏrŏbunŭn Han-guginimnida.
   여러분은 한국인입니다.
6. Yŏngŏrŭl hashimnikka?
   영어를 하십니까?
7. Kŭnŭn Miguk sarami animnida.
   그는 미국 사람이 아닙니다.

Family	*kajok* 가족	Father	*abŏji* 아버지	Mother	*ŏmŏni* 어머니
Brother	*hyŏng, tongsaeng* 형, 동생	Sister	*nui* 누이	Wife	*anae, ch'ŏ, puin* 아내, 처, 부인
Sweetheart	*aein* 애인	Friend	*ch'in-gu* 친구	Acquaintance	*ch'inji* 친지
Student	*haksaeng* 학생	Man	*namja* 남자	Woman	*yŏja* 여자

5. Additional Words and Expressions
Cassette—Side A

8. He's a French.
9. They are Japanese.
10. They are tourists.

8. Kŭnŭn P'ŭrangsŭ saramimnida.
   그는 프랑스 사람입니다.
9. Kŭdŭrŭn Ilbon saramimnida.
   그들은 일본 사람입니다.
10. Kŭdŭrŭn kwan-gwanggaegimnida.
    그들은 관광객입니다.

— B —

1. Pardon me.
   Excuse me.
2. Please forgive me.
3. May I help you?(1)
4. May I ask you a question?
5. May I ask you a favor?
6. May I come in?

1. Shillyehamnida.
   실례합니다.
2. Yongsŏhae chushipshio.
   용서해 주십시오.
3. Towa tŭrilkkayo?
   도와 드릴까요?
4. Malssŭm chom mutkessŭmnida.
   말씀 좀 묻겠습니다.
5. Put'ak chom tŭrigessŭmnida.
   부탁 좀 드리겠습니다.
6. Tŭrŏgado chossŭmnikka?
   들어가도 좋습니까?

---

(1) "May I help you?" may be used differently in Korean according to the situation.
  a. When one wants to help some one: *Towa tŭrilkkayo?* (도와 드릴까요?)
  b. At a restaurant or a shop counter: *Muŏsŭl tŭrilkkayo?* (What shall I { serve / give you? / show)
     (무엇을 드릴까요?)
  c. At office or home: *Ŏttŏk'e osyŏssŭmnikka?* (What brings you here?)
     (어떻게 오셨습니까?)

Part I
Cassette—Side A

7. May I use it?
8. What a fine day!
9. I'm very glad.
10. What a rain!
11. I'm discouraged.

7. Igŏsŭl ssŏdo chossŭmnikka?
   이것을 써도 좋습니까?
8. Nalssiga ch'am chok'unyo
   날씨가 참 좋군요.
9. Kibuni chossŭmnida.
   기분이 좋습니다.
10. Wen piga irŏk'e omnikka?
    웬 비가 이렇게 옵니까?
11. Shilmanghaessŭmnida.
    실망했습니다.

— C —

1. She's very kind.
2. I'm happy.
3. He's rude.
4. I'm angry.
5. I lost my bag.
6. That's too bad.
7. Come back soon.

1. Kŭ yŏjanŭn maeu ch'injŏrhamnida.
   그 여자는 매우 친절합니다.
2. Kippŭmnida.
   기쁩니다.
3. Kŭnŭn muryehamnida.
   그는 무례합니다.
4. Hwaga namnida.
   화가 납니다.
5. Paegŭl irobŏryŏssŭmnida.
   백을 잃어버렸습니다.
6. Ch'am andwaessŭmnida.
   참 안 됐습니다.
7. Kot toraoshipshio.
   곧 돌아오십시오.

5. Additional Words and Expressions
Cassette—Side A

8. Drop in anytime.

9. Call me up tomorrow.

10. Please come in.

11. Please sit down.

12. Please wait a moment.

8. Ŏnjedŭnji tŭllŭshipshio.
   언 제 든 지 들 르 십 시 오.

9. Naeil chŏnhwahashipshio.
   내 일 전 화 하 십 시 오.

10. Tŭrŏoshipshio.
    들 어 오 십 시 오.

11. Anjŭshipshio.
    앉 으 십 시 오.

12. Chamkkanman kidarishipshio.
    잠 깐 만 기 다 리 십 시 오.

Subway

Bank

Movie Theater

PART II
EVERYDAY CONVERSATION

1. Introduction
(Sogae : 소개)

Mr. Yun: Miss Smith, this is Mr. Kim, my friend.

M.Y: Sŭmisŭ yang, che ch'in-gu Kim kunimnida.
스미스 양,⁽¹⁾ 제 친구 김 군⁽²⁾입니다.

Miss Smith: How do you do, Mr. Kim. I'm glad to meet you.

M.S: Annyŏnghashimnikka, misŭt'ŏ Kim. Mannasŏ pan-gapsŭmnida.
안녕하십니까, 미스터 김?⁽³⁾ 만나서 반갑습니다.

* * *

Mr. Kim: President Im, may I introduce Miss Smith from America?

M.K: Im sajangnim, Migugesŏ oshin Sŭmisŭ yangŭl sogaehagessŭmnida.
임 사장님, 미국에서 오신 스미스 양을 소개하겠습니다.

---

(1) Standard Korean speech has little intonation—that is, rise and fall in pitch of voice, therefore, it may be spoken evenly with slight accent on syllables.

(2) 군 (*kun*) is a familiar title for one's male friends and inferiors. After one marries this title is usually dropped.

(3) The use of 씨 (*ssi*) is preferred with the full name for a male.

President Im: How do you do, Miss Smith? Please come in.

M.S: How do you do, President Im? Thank you very much for inviting me.

P.I: How long will you stay in Korea?

M.S: I'll stay about two months.

P.I: I hope you will enjoy your stay.

P.I: Annyŏnghashimnikka, Sŭmisŭ yang? Ŏsŏ oshipshio.
안녕하십니까, 스미스 양? 어서 오십시오. (4)

M.S: Annyŏnghashimnikka, Im sajangnim?
안녕하십니까, 임 사장님?
Ch'odaehae chusyŏsŏ kamsahamnida.
초대해 주셔서 감사합니다.

P.I: Han-guge ŏlma tongan kyeshil yejŏngimnikka?
한국에 얼마 동안 계실 예정입니까?

M.S: Han tu taltchŭm mŏmurŭlkka hamnida.
한 두 달쯤 머무를까 합니다.

P.I: Yŏgi kyeshinŭn tongan mani chŭlgishigi paramnida.
여기 계시는 동안 많이 즐기시기 바랍니다.

---

(4) This expression is customarily used on nearly all occasions where one receives guests, visitors or clients. (cf. Page 47)

2. Invitation
(Ch'odae : 초대)

Mr. Im: Hello, Miss Smith? How are you?

Miss Smith: Fine, thank you, and you?

M.I: I'm fine, too. By the way, Miss Smith, will you be free tomorrow evening?

M.S: Yes, I'll be free tomorrow. Why?

M.I: Well, my wife and I would like to have you dine with us

M.I: Yŏboseyo, Sŭmisŭ yangieyo?
여보세요, 스미스 양이에요?
Annyŏnghashimnikka?
안녕하십니까?

M.S: Ye, annyŏnghashimnikka?
예, 안녕하십니까?

M.I: Ye, kŭrŏnde Sŭmisŭ yang, naeil chŏnyŏge shigan issŭmnikka?
예, 그런데 스미스 양, 내일 저녁에 시간 있습니까?

M.S: Ye, naeil shigani issŭmnida.
예, 내일 시간이 있습니다.
Wae kŭrŏseyo?
왜 그러세요?

M.I: Chŏ, che anaewa kach'i tangshinŭl moshigo naeil chŏnyŏgŭl hago shipsŭmnida.

Part II
Cassette—Side B

tomorrow evening.⁽¹⁾

저, 제 아내와 같이 당신을 모시고 내일 저녁 을 하고 싶습니다.

M.S: Oh, that would be very nice. Where?

M.S: Ye, komapsŭmnida. Ŏdiesŏyo?
예, 고맙습니다. 어디에서요?

M.I: Can you come over to our house?

M.I: Chŏhŭi chibe oshil su issŭmnikka?
저희 집에 오실 수 있습니까?

M.S: Yes, certainly. What time shall I come?

M.S: Ye, myŏt shie kalkkayo?
예, 몇시에 갈까요?

M.I: How about six?

M.I: Yŏsŏssiga ŏttaeyo?
6시가 어때요?

M.S: Fine, I'll be there at six.

M.S: Ye, yŏsŏssie kagessŭmnida.
예, 6시에 가겠습니다.

M.I: Good. We'll be expecting you then.

M.I: Chossŭmnida, kŭrŏm kidarigessŭmnida.
좋습니다. 그럼 기다리겠습니다.

---

(1) this evening—*onŭl chŏnyŏk* (오늘 저녁)   this morning—*onŭl ach'im* (오늘 아침)   tomorrow morning—*naeil ach'im* (내일 아침)   yesterday evening—*ŏje chŏnyŏk* (어제 저녁)

3. Visit
(Pangmun : 방문)

At the Office

Secretary: May I help you?

Mr. Williams: I came to see President Im.
I have an appointment. My name is John Williams.

S.C: I'm sorry. He is not in right now. But he will be back soon. Please come in and wait.

M.W: Thank you.

S.C: Ŏttŏk'e osyŏssŭmnikka?
어떻게 오셨습니까?

M.W: Im sajangnimŭl poerŏ wassŭmnida.
임 사장님을 뵈러 왔습니다.
Yaksogŭl hayŏssŭmnida.
약속을 하였습니다.
Che irŭmŭn Chon Williŏmjŭimnida.
제 이름은 존 윌리엄즈입니다.

S.C: Mianhamnida, chigŭm an kyeshimnida.
미안합니다, 지금 안 계십니다.
Kŭrŏch'iman kot toraoshil kŏmnida.
Turŏwasŏ kidarishipshio.
그렇지만 곧 돌아오실 겁니다. 들어와서 기다리십시오.

M.W: Komapsŭmnida.
고맙습니다.

Part II
Cassette—Side B

(A Few Minutes Later)

President Im: Good afternoon Mr. Williams. I'm sorry to have kept you waiting.

Mr. Williams: That's all right. I came a little early.

P.I: Well, how was your trip?

M.W: Excellent.

P.I: Are you going to have time to do some sightseeing this time?

M.W: Yes. I want to visit the Secret Garden(Ch'angdŏkkung) tomorrow.

P.I: That's fine. I hope you will enjoy it very much.

P.I: Annyŏnghashimnikka, Williŏmjŭ ssi?
안녕하십니까, 윌리엄즈 씨?
Orae kidarige haesŏ mianhamnida.
오래 기다리게 해서 미안합니다.

M.W: Kwaench'anssŭmnida. Chega chom iltchik wassŭmnida.
괜찮습니다. 제가 좀 일찍 왔습니다.

P.I: Chŏ, p'yŏnhi osyŏssŭmnikka?
저, 편히 오셨습니까?

M.W: Ye, chal wassŭmnida.
예, 잘 왔습니다.

P.I: Ibŏnenŭn kugyŏnghashil shigani itkessŭmnikka?
이번에는 구경하실 시간이 있겠습니까?

M.W: Ne, naeil Piwŏne(Ch'angdŏkkung) karyŏmnida.
네, 내일 비원(창덕궁)에 가렵니다.

P.I: Ch'am chossŭmnida. Mani chŭlgishigi paramnida.
참 좋습니다. 많이 즐기시기 바랍니다.

4. Asking for Information
(Munnŭn mal : 묻는 말)

― A ―

Miss Smith: Excuse me. How do I get to Yonhui-dong?

Student: It is a little far from here. Take bus #8 and get off in front of the Seoul Foreign School.

M.S: Thank you.

S.T: You're welcome.

M.S: Mianhamnida.
미안합니다.
Yŏnhŭidonge ŏttŏk'e kamnikka?
연희동에 어떻게 갑니까?

S.T: Chom mŏmnida.
좀 멉니다.
P'albŏn pŏsŭrŭl t'ashigo Sŏul oegugin hakkyo ap'esŏ naerishipshio.
8번 버스를 타시고 서울 외국인 학교 앞에서 내리십시오.

M.S: Komapsŭmnida.
고맙습니다.

S.T: Ch'ŏnmaneyo.
천만에요.

― B ―

Miss Smith: Excuse me, but can you

M.S: Shillyehamnida.
실례합니다.

Part II
Cassette—Side B

tell me which house is No. 54?

Student: No. 54?
Go this way and then turn left at the drugstore.
No. 54 is the second house on the left.

S.T: Oshipsa pŏnjiga ŏnŭ chibimnikka?
54번지가 어느 집입니까?

S.T: Oshipsa pŏnjiyo?
54 번지요?
I killo kasyŏsŏ yakpangesŏ oentchogŭro toseyo.
이 길로 가셔서 약방에서 왼쪽으로 도세요.
Kŭrŏmyŏn oentchogŭro tu pŏntchaega kŭ chibimnida.
그러면 왼쪽으로 두 번째가 그 집입니다.

— C —

Mr. Williams: Where can I buy a map of Korea?

Student: You can get one in a bookstore.

M.W: Where is the nearest bookstore?

M.W: Han-guk chidorŭl ŏdisŏ sal su issŭmnikka?
한국 지도를 어디서 살 수 있습니까?

S.T: Ch'aekpangesŏ sal su issŭmnida.
책방에서 살 수 있습니다.

M.W: Cheil kakkaun ch'aekpangi ŏdi issŭmnikka?
제일 가까운 책방이 어디 있습니까?

4. Asking for Information
Cassette—Side B

S.T: Turn right at the first traffic light. Continue walking about 100 meters.
You will find several bookstores on your right.

M.W: Thank you very much.

S.T: Don't mention it.

S.T: Ch'ŏŭm shinho-esŏ orŭntchogŭro toseyo.
처음 신호에서 오른쪽으로 도세요.
Kŭrigo yak paek mit'ŏ kŏrŏgaseyo.
그리고 약 100미터 걸어가세요.
Orŭntchoge ch'aekpangi myŏt chip issŭmnida.
오른쪽에 책방이 몇 집 있습니다.

M.W: Taedanhi kamsahamnida.
대단히 감사합니다.

S.T: Ch'ŏnmanŭi malssŭmimnida.
천만의 말씀입니다.

Bookstore

5. Getting around in Town
(Shinaeŭi Kyot'ong : 시내의 교통)

(1) Taxi

Mr. Williams: Taxi! Taxi!

Taxi Driver: Please get in. Where to, sir?

M.W: Let's go to the Toksu Palace, please.

T.D: All right, sir.

M.W: Does it take long to get there?

T.D: Yes, it will take about twenty minutes.

M.W: Please drive carefully.

T.D: Yes, sir.

M.W: T'aekshi, t'aekshi!
택시, 택시!

T.D: Ŏsŏ t'aseyo.
어서 타세요.
Ŏdiro moshilkkayo?
어디로 모실까요?

M.W: Tŏksugungŭro kapshida.
덕수궁으로 갑시다.

T.D: Ye, arassŭmnida.
예, 알았습니다.

M.W: Orae kŏllimnikka?
오래 걸립니까?

T.D: Ye, han ishippun kŏllimnida.
예, 한 20분 걸립니다.

M.W: Choshimhae kaseyo.
조심해 가세요.

T.D: Ne, kŭrŏgessŭmnida.
네, 그러겠습니다.

5. Getting around in Town
Cassette—Side B

T.D: Here we are, sir.

M.W: How much do I owe you?

T.D: 900 won, sir.

Thank you. Good-bye sir.

* The fare is based on the basic minimum plus distance and time. The current basic fare is 1,300won.

T.D: Ta wassŭmnida.
다 왔습니다.

M.D: Ŏlmaimnikka?
얼마입니까?

T.D: Kubaegwŏnimnida.
900원입니다.
Komapsŭmnida. Annyŏnghi kaship-shio.
고맙습니다. 안녕히 가십시오.

(2) Bus

Mr. Williams: Tell me an interesting place to visit near Seoul.

Mr. Lee: Well, there is the Korean Folk Village at Suwon(Yongin).

M.W: How can I get there?

M.L: You can take one of the tourist buses which go there.

(At the Bus Terminal)

M.W: Which bus goes to the

M.W: Sŏul kŭnch'ŏe kabol manhan koshi ŏdiimnikka?
서울 근처에 가볼 만한 곳이 어디입니까?

M.L: Suwŏn (Yongin)e Han-guk minsokch'oni issŭmnida.
수원(용인)에 한국 민속촌이 있습니다.

M.W: Ŏttŏk'e kal su issŭmnikka?
어떻게 갈 수 있습니까?

M.L: Kŏgi kanŭn kwan-gwang pŏsŭrŭl t'ashipshio.
거기 가는 관광 버스를 타십시오.

M.W: Ŏnŭ pŏsŭga minsokch'one kamnikka?

Part II
Cassette—Side B

Korean Folk Village?

Attendant: This one leaves in five minutes. Did you buy your ticket?

M.W: No, not yet.

A.D: Get your ticket at window #5. Please, hurry.

M.W: Thank you.

A.D: I pŏsŭga obun hue ttŏnamnida.
이 버스가 5분 후에 떠납니다.
P'yorŭl sasyŏssŭmnikka?
표를 사셨습니까?

M.W: Anio, ajik an sassŭmnida.
아니오, 아직 안 샀습니다.

A.D: Chŏ obŏn ch'angguesŏ p'ani ŏsŏ sa-oseyo.
저 5번 창구에서 파니 어서 사오세요.[1]

M.W: Komapsŭmnida.
고맙습니다.

어느 버스가 민속촌에 갑니까?

(3) Subway

Mr. Williams: Where is the Daewoo Center?

A Passer-by: It's near the Seoul Railroad Station.

M.W: Taeu sent'ŏnŭn odi issŭmnikka?
대우 센터는 어디 있습니까?

P.B: Sŏullyŏk kŭnch'ŏe issŭmnida.
서울역 근처에 있습니다.

---

(1) It means as much as "Hurry to get one and come back!"

5. Getting around in Town
Cassette—Side B

M.W: How can I get there?

P.B: The subway is the best.

M.W: Oh yes. I've heard about it. Where's the nearest station?

P.B: There's an entrance right over there.
Get off at the Seoul Station. You'll get there in 15 minutes.

M.W: Thank you very much.

P.B: You're welcome

M.W: Ŏttŏk'e kal su issŭmnikka?
어떻게 갈 수 있습니까?

P.B: Chihach'ŏri cheil chossŭmnida.
지하철이 제일 좋습니다.

M.W: A, ne. Tŭrŭn chŏgi issŭmnida.
아, 네. 들은 적이 있습니다.
Kakkaun chŏnggŏjangi ŏdimnikka?
가까운 정거장이 어딥니까?

P.B: Paro chŏgi ipkuga issŭmnida.
바로 저기 입구가 있습니다.
Sŏullyŏgesŏ naeriseyo.
서울역에서 내리세요.
Shibobunimyŏn kal kŏmnida.
15분이면 갈 겁니다.

M.W: Taedanhi komapsŭmnida.
대단히 고맙습니다.

P.B: Ch'ŏnmaneyo.
천만에요.

6. Shopping
(Mulgŏnsagi : 물건사기)

(1) At a Department Store

Salesgirl: May I help you?

Mrs. Green: Yes, I want to see the handbag over there.

S.G: You mean the black one?

M.G: No, the brown one beside it.

S.G: Muŏsŭl tŭrilkkayo?
무엇을 드릴까요?

M.G: Ye, chŏgi chŏ paegŭl poyŏ chuseyo.
예, 저기 저 백을 보여 주세요.

S.G: I kkaman kŏt marimnikka?
이 까만 것 말입니까?

M.G: Anio, kŭ yŏp'ŭi kalsaek kŏt marimnida.
아니오, 그 옆의 갈색 것 말입니다.

* * *

M.G: It's very beautiful. How much is it?

S.G: It's 42,000 won.

M.G: I think that's too expensive.

M.G: Igŏt ch'am chok'unyo.
이것 참 좋군요.
Ŏlmaimnikka?
얼마입니까?

S.G: Samanich'ŏnwŏnimnida.
42,000원입니다.

M.G: Nŏmu pissagunyo.
너무 비싸군요.

6. Shopping

Do you have any cheaper ones?

S.G: How about this one, Ma'am? It's 34,000 won.

M.G: Good. I'll take it. Here's the money.

S.G: Here's your change. Thank you, Ma'am.

Tŏ ssan kŏt ŏpsŭmnikka?
더 싼 것 없습니까?

S.G: Igŏsŭn ŏttŏssŭmnikka, puin?
이것은 어떻습니까, 부인?
Igŏsŭn sammansach'ŏnwŏnimnida.
이것은 34,000원입니다.

M.G: Chossŭmnida. Igŏsŭl sajiyo.
좋습니다. 이것을 사지요.
Ton yŏgi issŭmnida.
돈 여기 있습니다.

S.G: Kŏsŭrŭmton yŏgi issŭmnida.
거스름돈 여기 있습니다.
Komapsŭmnida.
고맙습니다.

(2) At a Souvenir Shop

Salesclerk: Good afternoon. May I help you, sir?

Mr. Williams: Yes. I want to pick out some souvenirs for my friends.

S.C: Annyŏnghashimnikka, muŏsŭl tŭrilkkayo?
안녕하십니까, 무엇을 드릴까요?'

M.W: Ye, che ch'in-guege chul kinyŏmp'umŭl chom saryŏmnida.
예, 제 친구에게 줄 기념품을 좀 사렵니다.

Part II
Cassette—Side B

S.C: Please come in and look around.

S.C: Ŏsŏ tŭrŏwasŏ tullŏboseyo.
어서 들어와서 둘러보세요.

* * *

S.C: How about this lacquer ware?[1]

M.W: Good. I like these cigarette cases. How much are they?

S.C: These are 10,000 won each and those are 8,000 won.

M.W: Well, I want one for 10,000 won and two for 8,000 won. Please wrap them separately.

S.C: All right, sir.

S.C: I chagaenŭn ŏttŏssŭmnikka?
이 자개는 어떻습니까?

M.W: Chok'unyo. I tambaetkabi mame tŭrŏyo. Ŏlmajyo?
좋군요. 이 담뱃갑이 맘에 들어요. 얼마죠?

S.C: Igŏttŭrŭn manwŏnigo, chŏgŏttŭrŭn p'alch'ŏnwŏnimnida.
이것들은 10,000원이고 저것들은 8,000원입니다.

M.W: Kŭrŏm manwŏntchari hanawa p'alch'ŏnwŏntchari tul sagessŏyo. Ttaro ssa chuseyo.
그럼 10,000원짜리 하나와 8,000원짜리 둘 사겠어요. 따로 싸주세요.

S.C: Ye, arassŭmnida.
예, 알았습니다.

---

(1) Some typical souvenirs:
    amethyst—*chasujŏng* (자수정)   silk—*pidan* (비단)   silver ware—*ŭn-gi* (은기)
    china—*tojagi* (도자기)   wood carving—*mokkak* (목각)   brass—*notkŭrŭt* (놋그릇)

7. Telephone
(Chŏnhwa : 전화)

Mr. Williams: Hello, is this 335-4527?

Voice: Yes, it is.

M.W: May I talk to Mr. Song, please?

Voice: Who's calling, please?

M.W: This is John Williams.

Voice: Just a moment.

M.W: Yŏboseyo, kŏgiga samsamoŭi saoich'irimnikka?
여보세요, 거기가 335의 4527입니까?

VO: Ye, kŭrŏssŭmnida.
예, 그렇습니다.

M.W: Song sŏnsaengnim chom taejuseyo.
송 선생님 좀 대주세요.

VO: Nugushirago halkkayo?
누구시라고 할까요?

M.W: Chŏnŭn Chon Williŏmjŭimnida.
저는 존 윌리엄즈입니다.

VO: Chamkkanman kidarishipshio.
잠깐만 기다리십시오.

* * *

Mr. Song: Hello, Mr. Williams. How are you?

M.S: Annyŏnghashimnikka, Williŏmjŭ ssi?
안녕하십니까, 윌리엄즈 씨?

Part II
Cassette—Side B

Mr. Williams: Fine. May I see you now?
I want to plan my sightseeing tour.

M.S: Yes. certainly. Can you come over to the tearoom (coffee shop) in front of my office?

M.W: You mean the tearoom where we met, yesterday?

M.S: That's right.

M.W: O.K. I'll be there in fifteen minutes.

M.W: Ye, chom poeol su issŭlkkayo?
예, 좀 뵈올 수 있을까요?
Kwan-gwang kyehoegŭl seugo ship-sŭmnida.
관광 계획을 세우고 싶습니다.

M.S: Ye, chŏŭi samushil ap'ŭi tabangŭro (k'ŏp'isyop) oshil su issŭmnikka?
예, 저의 사무실 앞의 다방(커피숍)으로 오실 수 있습니까?

M.W: Uriga ŏjŏkke mannan kŭ tabang malssŭmimnikka?
우리가 어저께[1] 만난 그 다방 말씀입니까?

M.S: Kŭrŏssŭmnida.
그렇습니다.

M.W: Ye, shibobun naee kagessŭmnida.
예, 15분 내에 가겠습니다.

---

(1) Dates: today—*onŭl* (오늘) tomorrow—*naeil* (내일) the day after tomorrow—*more*, (모레)
yesterday—*ŏjŏkke* (어저께) the day before yesterday—*kŭjŏkke* (그저께)

8. At a Tearoom
(Tabangeso : 다방에서)

Hostess: Good morning. This way, please.

H.T: Ŏsŏ oseyo.[1]
어서 오세요.
Iriro oseyo.
이리로 오세요.

Mr. Song: How do you do, Mr. Williams?

M.S: Annyŏnghashimnikka, Williŏmjŭ ssi?
안녕하십니까, 윌리엄즈 씨?

Mr. Williams: I'm glad to see you again.

M.W: Tashi poepke toeŏ pan-gapsŭmnida.
다시 뵙게 되어 반갑습니다.

H.T: What would you like to drink?

H.T: Muŏsŭl tŭshigessŭmnikka?
무엇을 드시겠습니까?

M.S: Mr. Williams, would you care for a cup of Korean ginseng tea?

M.S: Williŏmjŭ ssi, Han-gugŭi insamch'arŭl tŭrŏ poshigessŭmnikka?
윌리엄즈 씨, 한국의 인삼차를 들어 보시겠습니까?

---

(1) Short form of *"Oso oshipshio."* (어서 오십시오.) meaning 'Welcome.' It is used when receiving a guest or client.

Part II
Cassette—Side B

M.W: Yes, I'd like to try it.

M.S: *(to hostess)* Two cups of ginseng tea, please.

H.T: Yes, sir. Do you take sugar in your tea?

M.S: No, there's no need for sugar.

M.W: This tea tastes very good. Now, let's plan our sightseeing tour.

M.W: Ne, masŭl pogo shipsŭmnida.
네, 맛을 보고 싶습니다.

M.S: Insamch'a tu chan chuseyo.
인삼차 두 잔 주세요.

H.T: Ye, sŏlt'ang nŏŏ tŭshigessŏyo?
예, 설탕 넣어 드시겠어요?

M.S: Anio, sŏlt'ang p'iryoŏpsŭmnida.
아니오, 설탕 필요없습니다.

M.W: Ch'amashi aju chossŭmnida.
차맛이 아주 좋습니다.
Cha, kŭrŏm uri kwan-gwang yŏhaeng kyehoegŭl seupshida.
자, 그럼 우리 관광 여행 계획을 세웁시다.

9. At a Palace
(Kogungesŏ : 고궁에서)

Mr. Williams: There are many interesting monuments in this palace.

Mr. Song: Yes, but there used to be many more.
Shall we visit the National Museum here, next?

M.W: That sounds good.

M.W: I kungenŭn chaemiinnŭn kŏnmuri mani issŭmnida.
이 궁에는 재미있는 건물이[1] 많이 있습니다.

M.S: Ye, hajiman chŏnenŭn tŏ manassŭmnida.
예. 하지만 전에는 더 많았습니다.
Taŭm kungnip pangmulgwanŭl polkkayo?
다음 국립 박물관을 볼까요?

M.W: Kŭrŏk'e hapshida.
그렇게 합시다.[2]

* * *

Mr. Williams: The museum is quite

M.W: Pangmulgwani aju chossŭmnida.
박물관이 아주 좋습니다.

---

(1) *kŏnmul* (건물 ; monuments) here refers only to the buildings.
(2) Literal translation would be, "Let's do so."

nice. I'm very much impressed by the collections.

Mr. Song: I'm glad you liked it.

M.W: Let's take a little rest over there by the pond.

M.S: All right. Let's.

M.W: Now, what shall we see this evening?

M.S: I would like to show you the panoramic view of Seoul this evening.

M.W: Fine. I'll be looking forward to it.

M.S: Sujipp'ume manŭn kammyŏngŭl padassŭmnida.
수집품에 많은 감명을 받았습니다.

M.S: Maŭme tŭshini kippŭmnida.
마음에 드시니 기쁩니다.

M.W: Chŏ yŏnmotka-esŏ chamkkan shwipshida.
저 연못가에서 잠깐 쉽시다.

M.S: Ye, kŭrŏk'e hapshida.
예, 그렇게 합시다.

M.W: Kŭrŏnde, onŭl chŏnyŏge muŏsŭl polkkayo?
그런데 오늘 저녁에 무엇을 볼까요?

M.S: Onŭl chŏnyŏgenŭn Sŏurŭi chŏn-gyŏngŭl poyŏ tŭrigessŭmnida.
오늘 저녁에는 서울의 전경을 보여 드리겠습니다.

M.W: Chossŭmnida. Chŏngmal kidaryŏjinun-gunyo.
좋습니다. 정말 기다려지는군요.

10. At a Pavilion
(Chŏngja-esŏ : 정자에서)

(Mr. Williams and Mr. Song ride up the Pugak Skyway.)

Mr. Williams: What a nice scenic drive!

M.W: I kil kyŏngch'iga ch'am chossŭmnida.
이 길 경치가 참 좋습니다.

Mr. Song: Here we are at the Octagonal Pavilion.

M.S: P'algakchŏnge ta wassŭmnida.
팔각정에 다 왔습니다.

* * *

M.S: It is particularly interesting here in the evening.

M.S: I kosŭn chŏnyŏkttaega tŏuk chossŭmnida.
이 곳은 저녁때가 더욱 좋습니다.

M.W: Yes, the lights and scenery are just enchanting.

M.W: Ye, chuwiŭi pulgwa kyŏngch'iga hwanghorhamnida.
예, 주위의 불과 경치가 황홀합니다.

M.W: Hum, now I have a full view of Seoul below me.
I never imagined that Seoul would be so beautiful at night.

M.S: Yes, but Seoul is a little crowded.

M.W: That's true.

M.W: Hŭm, ije Sŏuri hannune poinŭn-gunyo.
흠, 이제 서울이 한눈에 보이는군요.
Sŏurŭi pami irŏk'e arŭmdaunji mollassŭmnida.
서울의 밤이 이렇게 아름다운지 몰랐습니다.

M.S: Ye, kŭrŏch'iman Sŏurŭn chom pokchap'amnida.
예, 그렇지만 서울은 좀 복잡합니다.

M.W: Kŭgŏn sashirimnida.
그건 사실입니다.

* * *

M.S: Tomorrow, the bus for Kyongju will leave at nine-thirty. So, don't be late.

M.W: Don't worry. I'm an early riser.

M.S: Naeirŭn Kyŏngju kanŭn pŏsŭga ahopshi pane ttŏnamnida.
내일은 경주 가는 버스가 9시 반에 떠납니다.
Kŭrŏni nŭtchi mashipshio.
그러니 늦지 마십시오.

M.W: Yŏmnyŏ maseyo.
염려 마세요.
Chŏnŭn iltchik irŏnamnida.
저는 일찍 일어납니다.

11. At a Hotel
(Hot'ereso : 호텔에서)

Mr. Williams: Do you have two single rooms?

Clerk: Yes, we do, sir. The room on the 3rd floor is 30,000 won and the one on the 10th floor is 25,000 won.

M.W: How do you think Mr. Song?

Mr. Song: The room on the tenth

M.W: Tokpang tul issŭmnikka?
독방⁽¹⁾ 둘 있습니까?

C.K: Ne, samch'ŭng pangŭn samman-wŏnigo, shipch'ŭng pangŭn iman-och'ŏnwŏnimnida.
네, 3층 방은 30,000원이고 10층 방은 25,000원입니다.
* The current fare ranges from 100,000won to 150,000won.

M.W: Ŏttŏk'e saenggak'ashimnikka, Song sŏnsaengnim?
어떻게 생각하십니까, 송 선생님?

M.S: Shipch'ŭng pangŭn kyŏngch'iga tŏ

---

(1) a private room—*tokpang* (독방)   a western style room—*yangshil* (양실)
  a big room—*k'un pang* (큰 방)   a small room—*chagun pang* (작은 방)
  an ondol room (floor heated)—*ondolpang* (온돌방)

floor may have better view.

M.W: Then, we will take the rooms on the tenth.

C.K: Fine. Please fill in these forms. The bellboy will show you the rooms.

choŭl kŏmnida.
10층 방은 경치가 더 좋을 겁니다.

M.W: Kŭrŏmyŏn shipch'ŭng pange tŭljiyo.
그러면 10층 방에 들지요.

C.K: Chossŭmnida. I yongjie kiip'ae chuseyo.
좋습니다. 이 용지에 기입해 주세요.
Pangŭl annaehae tŭrigessŭmnida.
방을 안내해 드리겠습니다.

₩10,000 ₩5,000
₩1,000   ₩500   ₩100
         ₩50   ₩10

Denomination of Korean Currency

12. At a Restaurant
(Shiktangesŏ : 식당에서)

(Returning from a sightseeing tour)

Mr. Song: That was a long walk today, wasn't it?

Mr. Williams: Yes, it was.
I'm tired and a little hungry. Let's have a good dinner some place.

M.S: Would you like to have pulgogi this evening?

M.W: Yes, I'd love it.

M.S: O.K. Then, let's try that restaurant over there.

M.S: Onŭl mani kŏrŏssŭmnida.
오늘 많이 걸었습니다.
Kŭrŏch'iyo?
그렇지요?

M.W: Ne, kŭrŏssŭmnida.
네, 그렇습니다.
Chom p'igonhago paedo kop'ŭmnida.
좀 피곤하고 배도 고픕니다.
Ŏdi kasŏ chŏnyŏgŭl chal hapshida.
어디 가서 저녁을 잘 합시다.

M.S: Onŭl chŏnyŏk pulgogi hashigessŭmnikka?
오늘 저녁 불고기 하시겠습니까?

M.W: Ye, kŭgŏt ch'am chok'essŭmnida.
예, 그것 참 좋겠습니다.

M.S: Kŭrŏm, chŏgi chŏ shiktange kaboshipshida.
그럼, 저기 저 식당에 가보십시다.

Part II
Cassette—Side B

At a Table

Waiter: Are you ready to order now, sir?

W.T: Chumunhashigessŭmnikka?
주문하시겠습니까?

Mr. Song: Yes, bring us pulgogi, please.
Now, Mr. Williams, would you like naengmyon after pulgogi?

M.S: Ye, pulgogi kajyŏoseyo.
예, 불고기 가져오세요.
Pulgogi hashigo naengmyŏnŭl tŭshigessŭmnikka?
불고기 하시고 냉면을 드시겠습니까?

Mr. Williams: That must be wonderful. I like naengmyon very much.

M.W: Kŭgŏt ch'am chok'etkunyo.
그것 참 좋겠군요.
Chŏn naengmyŏnŭl maeu choahamnida.
전 냉면을 매우 좋아합니다.

M.S: *(to the waiter)* And two naengmyon later.

M.S: Kŭrŏmyŏn hue naengmyŏn tu kŭrŭshio.
그러면 후에 냉면 두 그릇이오.

W.T: Yes, sir. What would you like to drink?

W.T: Ne, muŏsŭl mashigessŭmnikka?
네, 무엇을 마시겠습니까?

12. At a Restaurant
Cassette—Side B

M.S: Mr. Williams, would you like to try the wine called Popchu? It's a specialty of Kyongju?

M.W: That'll be fine. I've heard a lot about it, but I've never tasted it.

M.S: Bring us a bottle of Popchu, too.

W.T: Yes, sir.

M.S: Williŏmjŭ ssi, pŏpchurŭl tŭrŏ poshigessŭmnikka?
윌리엄즈 씨, 법주를 들어 보시겠습니까?
Kyŏngjuŭi t'ŭksanimnida.
경주의 특산입니다.

M.W: Kŭgŏt ch'am chok'essŭmnida.
그것 참 좋겠습니다.
Iyaginŭn mani tŭrŏnnŭnde ajik masŭl mot poassŭmnida.
이야기는 많이 들었는데 아직 맛을 못 보았습니다.

M.S: Pŏpchudo han pyŏng kajyŏoseyo.
법주도 한 병 가져오세요.

W.T: Ne, arassumnida.
네, 알았습니다.

13. At the Post Office
(Uch'egusesŏ : 우체국에서)

Mr. Williams: I want to send these letters to America. How much postage do I have to put on them?

Clerk: By air, sir?

M.W: Yes, by air, please.

C.K: A first class letter is 440 won. A post card is 350 won.

* Nowadays a first class letter is 570won.

M.W: All right. Give me five 440 won stamps, and three 350

M.W: I p'yŏnjirŭl Miguge ponaeryŏmnida.
이 편지를 미국에 보내렵니다.
Up'yorŭl ŏlma puch'yŏya hamnikka?
우표를 얼마 붙여야 합니까?

C.K: Hanggongimnikka?
항공입니까?

M.W: Ye, hanggongŭroyo.
예, 항공으로요.

C.K: Ilchong p'yŏnjinŭn sabaeksashibwŏnimnida.
1종 편지는 440원입니다.
Yŏpsŏnŭn sambaegoshibwŏnimnida.
엽서는 350원입니다.

M.W: Kŭrŏm sabaeksashibwŏntchari tasŏt changhago, sambaegoshipwŏn tchari
그럼 440원짜리 다섯 장하고, 350원짜리

13. At the Post Office
Cassette—Side B

won stamps.

C.K: Here you are, sir.

M.W: And, I want to send these packages to England.

C.K: Please, take them to window #1.

M.W: Thank you.

sŏk chang chuseyo.
석장⁽¹⁾ 주세요.

C.K: Yŏgi issŭmnida.
여기 있습니다.

M.W: Kŭrigo i sop'orŭl Yŏngguge ponaeryŏmnida.
그리고, 이 소포를 영국에 보내렵니다.

C.K: Ilbŏn ch'anggue kajyŏgaseyo.
1번 창구에 가져가세요.

M.W: Komapsŭmnida.
고맙습니다.

Post Office

Public Telephone

Drugstore and Real Estate Agency

Tearoom and Barbershop

Inn

Beauty Parlor

APPENDIX

TO HELP UNDERSTAND KOREA

1. Romanization of the Korean Alphabet
(Based on the Ministry of Education System)

1. Vowels

ㅏ	ㅑ	ㅓ	ㅕ	ㅗ	ㅛ	ㅜ	ㅠ	ㅡ	ㅣ	ㅐ
a	ya	ŏ	yŏ	o	yo	u	yu	ŭ	i	ae

ㅒ	ㅔ	ㅖ	ㅚ	ㅟ	ㅢ	ㅘ	ㅙ	ㅝ	ㅞ
yae	e	ye	oe	wi	ŭi	wa	wae	wŏ	we

2. Consonants

ㄱ	ㄴ	ㄷ	ㄹ	ㅁ	ㅂ	ㅅ	ㅇ	ㅈ	ㅊ	ㅋ
k	n	t(d)	r(l)	m	p(b)	s	ng	ch(j)	ch'	k'

ㅌ	ㅍ	ㅎ	ㄲ	ㄸ	ㅃ	ㅆ	ㅉ
t'	p'	h	kk	tt	pp	ss	tch

3. Syllabary

가	갸	거	겨	고	교	구	규	그	기	개	걔	게
k(g)a	kya	kŏ	kyŏ	ko	kyo	ku	kyu	kŭ	ki	kae	kyae	ke

계	괴	귀	긔	과	괘	궈	궤
kye	koe	kwi	kŭi	kwa	kwae	kwŏ	kwe

나	냐	너	녀	노	뇨	누	뉴	느	니	내	냬	네
na	nya	nŏ	nyŏ	no	nyo	nu	nyu	nŭ	ni	nae	nyae	ne

녜	뇌	뉘	늬	놔	놰	눠	눼
nye	noe	nwi	nŭi	nwa	nwae	nwŏ	nwe

다	댜	더	뎌	도	됴	두	듀	드	디	대	댸	데
t(d)a	tya	tŏ	tyŏ	to	tyo	tu	tyu	tŭ	ti	tae	tyae	te
데	되	뒤	듸	돠	돼	뒈	뒈					
tye	toe	twi	tŭi	twa	twae	twŏ	twe					

라	랴	러	려	로	료	루	류	르	리	래	럐	레
r(l)a	rya	rŏ	ryŏ	ro	ryo	ru	ryu	rŭ	ri	rae	ryae	re
레	뢰	뤼	릐	롸	뢔	뤄	뤠					
rye	roe	rwi	rŭi	rwa	rwae	rwŏ	rwe					

마	먀	머	며	모	묘	무	뮤	므	미	매	먜	메
ma	mya	mŏ	myŏ	mo	myo	mu	myu	mŭ	mi	mae	myae	me
몌	뫼	뮈	믜	뫄	뫠	뭐	뭬					
mye	moe	mwi	mŭi	mwa	mwae	mwŏ	mwe					

바	뱌	버	벼	보	뵤	부	뷰	브	비	배	뱨	베
p(b)a	pya	pŏ	pyŏ	po	pyo	pu	pyu	pŭ	pi	pae	pyae	pe
폐	뵈	뷔	븨	봐	봬	붜	붸					
pye	poe	pwi	pŭi	pwa	pwae	pwŏ	pwe					

사	샤	서	셔	소	쇼	수	슈	스	시	새	섀	세
sa	sya	sŏ	syŏ	so	syo	su	syu	sŭ	shi	sae	syae	se
셰	쇠	쉬	싀	솨	쇄	숴	쉐					
sye	soe	shwi	sŭi	swa	swae	swŏ	swe					

아	야	어	여	오	요	우	유	으	이	애	얘	에
a	ya	ŏ	yŏ	o	yo	u	yu	ŭ	i	ae	yae	e
예	외	위	의	와	왜	워	웨					
ye	oe	wi	ŭi	wa	wae	wŏ	we					

1. Romanization of the Korean Alphabet

자	쟈	저	져	조	죠	주	쥬	즈	지	재	쟤	제
ch(j)a	chya	chŏ	chyŏ	cho	chyo	chu	chyu	chŭ	chi	chae	chyae	che
졔	죄	쥐	즤	좌	좨	줘	줴					
chye	choe	chwi	chŭi	chwa	chwae	chwŏ	chwe					

차	챠	처	쳐	초	쵸	추	츄	츠	치	채	챼	체
ch'a	ch'ya	ch'ŏ	ch'yŏ	ch'o	ch'yo	ch'u	ch'yu	ch'ŭ	ch'i	ch'ae	ch'yae	ch'e
쳬	최	취	츼	촤	쵀	춰	췌					
ch'ye	ch'oe	ch'wi	ch'ŭi	ch'wa	ch'wae	ch'wŏ	ch'we					

카	캬	커	켜	코	쿄	쿠	큐	크	키	캐	컈	케
k'a	k'ya	k'ŏ	k'yŏ	k'o	k'yo	k'u	k'yu	k'ŭ	k'i	k'ae	k'yae	k'e
켸	쾨	퀴	킈	콰	쾌	쿼	퀘					
k'ye	k'oe	k'wi	k'ŭi	k'wa	k'wae	k'wŏ	k'we					

타	탸	터	텨	토	툐	투	튜	트	티	태	턔	테
t'a	t'ya	t'ŏ	t'yŏ	t'o	t'yo	t'u	t'yu	t'ŭ	t'i	t'ae	t'yae	t'e
톄	퇴	튀	틔	톼	퇘	퉈	퉤					
t'ye	t'oe	t'wi	t'ŭi	t'wa	t'wae	t'wŏ	t'we					

파	퍄	퍼	펴	포	표	푸	퓨	프	피	패	퍠	페
p'a	p'ya	p'ŏ	p'yŏ	p'o	p'yo	p'u	p'yu	p'ŭ	p'i	p'ae	p'yae	p'e
폐	푀	퓌	픠	퐈	퐤	풔	풰					
p'ye	p'oe	p'wi	p'ŭi	p'wa	p'wae	p'wŏ	p'we					

하	햐	허	혀	호	효	후	휴	흐	히	해	햬	헤
ha	hya	hŏ	hyŏ	ho	hyo	hu	hyu	hŭ	hi	hae	hyae	he
혜	회	휘	희	화	홰	훠	훼					
hye	hoe	hwi	hŭi	hwa	hwae	hwŏ	hwe					

2. The Korean Alphabet and Pronunciation

The Korean Alphabet, Hun Min Chǒng Ǔm (훈민정음) was invented by King Sejong of the Yi Dynasty more than five centuries ago.

There are 21 vowels and 19 consonants provided under the structure of the Korean Alphabet of 24 letters, 14 consonants and 10 vowels.

Vowels: ㅏ ㅑ ㅓ ㅕ ㅗ ㅛ ㅜ ㅠ ㅡ ㅣ ㅐ ㅔ ㅚ ㅢ ㅝ ㅖ ㅒ ㅟ ㅟ ㅘ ㅙ

Consonants: ㄱ ㄴ ㄷ ㄹ ㅁ ㅂ ㅅ ㅇ ㅈ ㅊ ㅋ ㅌ ㅍ ㅎ ㄲ ㄸ ㅃ ㅆ ㅉ

1. *Vowel Sounds*

The vowels of the Korean Alphabet are classified in the writing form into two categories,

Simple Vowels				Compound Vowels			
Korean	English Sounds	Korean	English Sounds	Korean	English Sounds	Korean	English Sounds
아 a	as ah	야 ya	as yard	애 ae	as at	얘 yae	as yam
어 ŏ	approximately as saw	여 yŏ	approximately yearn	에 e	as met	예 ye	as yes
오 o	as oh	요 yo	as yoke	외 oe	as Köln	위 wi	as we
우 u	as do	유 yu	as you	의 ŭi	approximately taken + we	와 wa	as wander
으 ŭ	approximately taken			워 wŏ	as water	왜 wae	as WAC
이 i	as ink			웨 we	as wet		

simple and compound.

The English sounds given here are, of course, approximate ones.

"ㅇ" in the above table is classified under consonants, but it is silent at the beginning of a letter. The rules to form a syllable will be explained in the page 71.

2. *Consonant Sounds*

1. Simple Consonants

Korean	English Sounds	Korean	English Sounds	Korean	English Sounds
ㄱ k/g	k or g as king or grocer (lightly aspirated)	ㅂ p/b	p or b as pin or book (lightly aspirated)	ㅋ k'	k as kite
ㄴ n	n as name	ㅅ s	s as same (lightly pronounced)	ㅌ t'	t as tank
ㄷ t/d	t or d as toy or depend (lightly aspirated)	ㅇ o	o or ng as ah or king	ㅍ p'	p as pump
ㄹ r/l	l or r as rain or lily	ㅈ ch/j	ch or j as John	ㅎ h	h high
ㅁ m	m as mother	ㅊ ch'	ch as church	There are no f's, v's and z's in Korean sounds

2. Double Consonants

a. For initial or final positions

These are pronounced stronger than single counterpart.

Korean	English Sounds	Korean	English Sounds	Korean	English Sounds
ㄲ kk	(kk) as sky or Jack	ㅃ pp	(pp) as spy	ㅉ tch	(jj) as joy with a strong emphasis
ㄸ tt	(tt) as stay	ㅆ ss	(ss) as essence		

b. For final positions only

These consonants will have full sound values depending on the word that follows.

Korean	English Sounds	Korean	English Sounds	Korean	English Sounds	Korean	English Sounds
ㄳ	ks(h) Ex. 넋	ㄺ	lk Ex. 읽다	ㄾ	rt' Ex. 핥다	ㅄ	ps Ex. 값
ㄵ	nj Ex. 앉다	ㄻ	lm Ex. 삶다	ㄿ	lp' Ex. 읖다	ㄽ	ls(h) Ex. 돐
ㄶ	nh Ex. 많다	ㄼ	lb Ex. 밟다	ㅀ	lh Ex. 싫다		

3. Sound Changes

Some sound changes take place when the words are linked together.
The following table⁽¹⁾ will give you a convenient guideline.

Final \ Initial	ㅇ	ㄱ K	ㄴ N	ㄷ T	ㄹ (R)	ㅁ M	ㅂ P	ㅅ S	ㅈ ch,j	ㅊ ch'	ㅋ k'	ㅌ t'	ㅍ p'	ㅎ h
ㄱ	k	g	kk	ngn	kt	ngn	ngm	kp	ks	kch	kch'	kk'	kt'	kp'	k'
ㄴ	n	n	n-g	nn	nd	ll	nm	nb	ns	nj	nch'	nk'	nt'	np'	nh
ㄹ	l	r	lg	ll	lt	ll	lm	lb	ls	lj	lch'	lk'	lt'	lp'	rh
ㅁ	m	m	mg	mn	md	mn	mm	mb	ms	mj	mch'	mk'	mt'	mp'	mh
ㅂ	p	b	pk	mn	pt	mn	mm	pp	ps	pch	pch'	pk'	pt'	pp'	p'
ㅇ	ng	ng	ngg	ngn	ngd	ngn	ngm	ngb	ngs	ngj	ngch'	ngk'	ngt'	ngp'	ngh

(1) Adopted from the simplified table by McCune-Reischauer.

4. *Rule to Form a Syllable*

The Korean Alphabet is not used like the English Alphabet. The Korean Alphabet is used to build up separate syllables.

For example, ㄱ + ㅏ = 가   ㄱ + ㅏ + ㅁ = 감
                  k   a   ka   k   a   m kam

The general rule is:

| Consonant *or* Silent "ㅇ" | + | Vowel | + | Consonant |

More examples:

Korean Letter Complete Syllable	Initial Consonant	Vowel	Consonant	Pronounced
아	ㅇ (Silent)	ㅏ	none	<u>ah</u>
너	ㄴ	ㅓ	none	as <u>non</u>sense
씨	ㅆ	ㅣ	none	as <u>se</u>at
산	ㅅ	ㅏ	ㄴ	<u>san</u>
흙	ㅎ	ㅡ	ㄺ	<u>hŭk</u>
땅	ㄸ	ㅏ	ㅇ	<u>ttang</u>
꿩	ㄲ	ㅝ	ㅇ	<u>kkwŏng</u>

5. *Table of Pronouns*

English	Korean	English	Korean
I	nanŭn (*or* naega)	He	kŭnŭn (*or* kŭga)
We	urinŭn (*or* uriga)	His	kŭŭi
My	naŭi	Him	kŭrŭl (*or* kŭege)
Our	uriŭi[1]	She	kŭyŏjaga (*or* kŭyŏjanŭn)
Me	na-ege (*or* narŭl)	Her	kŭyŏjaŭi
Us	uriege (*or* urirŭl)	Her	kŭyŏjarŭl (*or* kŭyŏja-ege)
You	tangshinŭn (*or* tangshini)	They	kŭdŭrŭn (*or* kŭdŭri)
Your	tangshinŭi	Their	kŭdŭrŭi
You	tangshinege (*or* tangshinŭl)	Them	kŭdŭrege (*or* kŭdŭrŭl)

3. Land and People

Korea is a mountainous peninsula, which in overall size is approximately equivalent to the state of New York or Great Britain.

The northern zone of the nation, occupied successively by Soviet military forces and a Communist dictatorship since 1945, comprises 122,370 square *km* while the Republic of Korea to the south is slightly smaller, with 98,445 square *km*.

The nation's climate is temperate. The hottest months are July and August; the coldest, December and January. The rainy season begins in June and ends in August. During this period, on an average of 50%

---

(1) In Korean conversation *uri* ' 우리 ' (meaning 'our') is often intimately used to mean my house, my brother and so on instead of *naŭi* (나의), *chŏŭi* (저의) or *che* (제).

of the total yearly precipitation is recorded.

Koreans, although descendants of several Mongol tribal groups which migrated from the north in the prehistoric times, were early fused into a separate, homogeneous race, independent of their neighbors, with traits distinctive from both the Chinese and Japanese.

Basic thing among these perhaps is language. Koreans all speak and write the same language. This is an important factor for spirit of national unity and solidarity, which has been especially characteristic of Koreans for centuries.

The population of the Republic of Korea exceeded 50 million in 1984 and that of the communist North Korea is presumably around 18 million.

4. History

Ancient Korean history goes back to the legendary Tan-gun a mythical divine being, who is said to have descended from heaven to assume leadership of primitive clans and tribes in 2333 B.C.

The first documented histories describe the rise and fall of the Three Kingdoms:

Koguryŏ (37 B.C.—668 A.D.) in southern Manchuria and northern Korea, Paekche (18 B.C.—660 A.D.) around the Han River basin, and Shilla (57 B.C.—936 A.D.) in the southern part of Korea along the Naktong.

The kings and generals of the Shilla finally united all Korea and settled the country roughly in the present size. The people could concentrate on culture. They built observatories, and magnificent temples, modeled Buddhist sculpture, and invented musical instruments, including exquisite jade flutes and the Korean harp called the Kayagŭm. The first ruler of the Koryŏ Dynasty came to the throne in 918 A.D. He inaugurated an era of enlightenment similar to that of King Alfred in England. In this era skilled craftsmen produced some of Korea's finest porcelain and built some of the greatest Buddhist monasteries.

Modern Seoul

The Yi Dynasty, dating from 1392, ushered in a golden age, similar to the Elizabethan era in England. Universities were founded, literature and the arts flourished. Books were printed from movable type about a half century before the Gutenberg Bible. The Yi Dynasty ended in 1910 when the Japanese, after years of encroachment, annexed Korea.

When World War II started the Japanese intensified their exploitation of Korea. But President Roosevelt, Prime Minister Churchill, and Generalissimo Chiang Kai-shek met in Cairo in 1943 and agreed that "in due course, Korea shall become free and independent."

Korea was liberated from Japanese tyranny in 1945 and the Republic was established in 1948. In 1950 Communist forces attacked in full force and sixteen countries of the UN participated in the War. "The Korean War," said President Rhee, "was fought not only for Koreans themselves... but also for the peace and security of mankind."

In 1960 Syngman Rhee, President of the Republic, responded to massive public demonstration and resigned. The government was replaced in 1961 by a military government. In 1963 the Third Republic was formed and Park Chung Hee was elected President.

In 1981, Chun Doo Hwan was formally elected President of the Fifth Republic under the new constitution. In his inaugural address, he pledged to build a democratic welfare society of Korea.

5. Holidays

New Year's Day is still celebrated according to the ancient Lunar Calendar, which places it in February most often. Members of the family get up early, put on their best clothes, and bow to parents or grandparents as reaffirmation of family ties. Small gifts

Preparation for New Year's Day

of food or money are given to children. Later, calls are made and received between branches of the family or close friends. (A person in mourning may receive visitors, but does not pay calls.)

Most of the traditional holidays relate to the seasonal farming cycle, and are thus also calculated by the old Lunar Calendar.

Talmaji hails the first full moon of the new year with torchlight parades and hillside bonfires. This was originally a fertility rite.

Hanshik, the hundred and fifth day after the winter solstice is hanshik, or cold food day, when people offer tributes of wine and food at their ancestors' graves. The food is not left to waste, for the family eats it later, picnic style.

Buddha's Birthday is on the eighth day of the fourth month, and is celebrated among believers with solemn processions bearing banners and lanterns, which also are used to adorn shrines and private houses.

Tano, the fifth day of the fifth month, is another occasion when food is offered to the household shrines of the ancestors. Also there are sports events, visits and feasts.

Ch'usŏk is the harvest festival which comes in the eighth month on the day when the moon is full. This time of abundance is still the gayest holiday of the year, although it, too, begins with solemn visits to tend the family grave sites and to intone prayers and present food offerings. After that are harvest dances with raucous village bands, lots of good food and wine to eat.

Tongji is the winter solstice. On this day, housewives cook red beans in porridge and soup, as well as cakes of glutinous rice. In olden days, new calendars used to be distributed on this holiday.

International holidays observed in Korea are Christmas, and Western New Year's.

The ancient traditional holidays may still be celebrated in the old ways in the countryside. Modern urban Koreans vary in their manner of observance, however, some will follow the dietary customs out of habit or nostalgia; some will pay tribute to ancestors' graves at the proper times, if they can; and others, an increasing proportion, simply use the free time for family or social activities, going to a movie, or having a night out.

6. A Few More Interesting Points

A. **100-day Celebration** (for a baby)

On the 100th day after birth, a celebration is held. The reason for the celebration is perhaps, that a child who has survived the first hundred days is likely to continue to survive.

Prepared rice cake are usually distributed to relatives and neighbors who sometimes give thread in return, which signifies longevity.

The gifts on the 100-day celebration are childrens' clothes, gold rings and other childrens' goods. In case one is invited to a celebration feast at home, it is customary to take a gift.

B. **Kunghap** (marriage custom)

If a parent is satisfied with the prospective bride or groom, the parent, preferably of the groom's family, go to a diviner's house to check whether the two will be a good match on the basis of the dates of birth. The custom is called Kunghap, which is still prevalent among many people. The matching of a couple is usually divined on the basis of the year, month, day and hour of one's birth to find out what the chances are

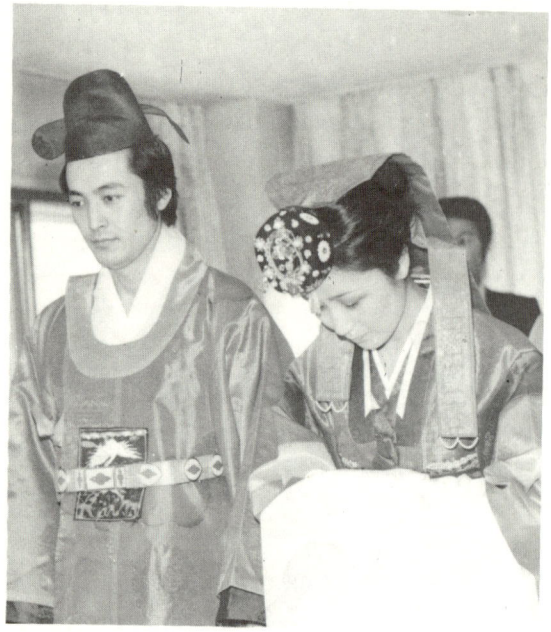
Bride and Groom

for happiness, prosperity and success, according to the old Chinese philosophy called 'ohaeng' (five elements).

C. **Chŏl** (Korean bows)

The Korean bows are generally divided into three types; the slight bow, the deep bow, and the traditional bow. The slight bow is usually performed in a casual manner among men, women and children on the street, at home or at school. The deep bow is not frequently seen in the cities. In the countryside, men as well as women, however, bow deeper than the slight bow. The traditional bow (chŏl) is no longer a common salutation as it used to be in the olden days. But on special occasions such as new year's greeting, memorial services for the ancestors and weddings, Koreans bow in the traditional way. To make a bow, a man places the palms of his hands flat on the floor in a triangular shape as he bends his body down; he touches the floor with his left knee and then with the right one.

D. **Kimch'i** (a spicy vegetable food)

Kimch'i is an indispensable food for Koreans throughout the four seasons. Consequently, Korean housewives spend a great deal of time and money to make it available for everyday meals. There are various kinds of kimch'i which are made according to the seasons. In the summer, 'yŏlmu' kimch'i is popular and in autumn, 'paech'u' kimch'i is usually prepared. In November and December when 'Kimjang' or the preparation of 'kimch'i' for the winter season starts,

6. A Few More Interesting Points

every market is filled with cabbages and turnips which attract bargaining housewives.

E. **Pulgogi** (seasoned charcoal broiled beef)

The broiled beef is perhaps one of the most popular and tastiest foods among the dishes at a formal dinner. It is thinly sliced beef seasoned with soy sauce, green onion, garlic, sesame oil, and sugar. In serving pulgogi, a clay fire pot with glowing charcoal in it is placed in the center of the table. Then a spherical shaped brass pan with holes in it is placed on top of the fire pot to broil the beef.

F. **Ondol** (hot floor of the house)

The ondol floor is made of slabs of granite laid over flues. To protect the room from smoke and to make a smooth floor, clay or cement must be placed over the stones, and paper, treated with bean oil, is pasted on to finish the ondol. The ondol is heated by wood and coal briquette and holds the heat for several hours even after the fire dies out.

The Spicy Cabbage Dish, Kimch'i

The Broiled Beef, Pulgogi

Ch'angdŏkkung